How to Make Your Own Books

Other books by Harvey Weiss

The Gadget Book
Motors and Engines and How They Work
Ship Models and How to Build Them

How to Make Your Own Books

Illustrated with Photographs and Drawings

by Harvey Weiss

THOMAS Y. CROWELL COMPANY   NEW YORK

Manufactured in the United States of America

ISBN 0–690–00400–1

Library of Congress Cataloging in Publication Data
Weiss, Harvey.
   How to make your own books.
   SUMMARY: Basic instructions for making a book accompany suggestions for special types of book-making projects—travel journals, diaries, photo albums, scrapbooks, comic books, and others.
   1. Books—Juv. lit. [1. Books] I. Title.
Z4.Z9W44   686   73–17267
ISBN 0–690–00400–1

10   9   8   7   6   5   4   3   2   1

Contents

Introduction

This book is about books—not the printed books you find in libraries, bookstores, or classrooms, but the personal, one-of-a-kind book. The books we are concerned with are diaries, stamp albums, travel journals, flip books, comic books, and several kinds of off-beat, experimental books.

In many cases something as simple as a four-page folder may do for a particular purpose. Or maybe a group of several four-page folders, sewn or stapled together, is what you need for a certain project. In other cases a long roll of paper or an "accordion"-folded sheet of paper might be what you want. All these things are referred to rather loosely as *books*, even though that is not the usual use of the word.

The large, hard-covered, cloth-, or leatherbound volume is not our interest here. That kind of bookbinding is a quite difficult, tricky business that requires special tools and skills and is another matter all together.

This book is divided into two parts. The first part is about practical matters. It explains different kinds of paper and different methods of folding, glueing, binding, attaching covers, and so on. The various ways of cutting and assembling paper to get the size and number of pages you want are discussed.

The second part is about the various uses or purposes of your personal book. There are ideas and suggestions for many different projects.

part one HOW IT'S DONE

1 / Kinds of Paper

The basic ingredient of any book is, of course, paper. There is an enormous variety of papers, and the kind you use will have a great deal to do with the sort of results you get. If you use thin, soiled, flimsy paper, or coarse drawing paper from an old pad that looks and feels like the paper used in newspapers, you will end up with a messy book that will tear easily and be hard to work with.

If, on the other hand, you get some crisp, clean, strong paper the entire feeling of the book will be different. You can't help but be influenced by the materials you use. Good materials will go a long way toward producing good results. In general, the sort of paper that this book is printed on, or perhaps a little heavier, is suitable for most of the personal books that we are discussing.

Where will you find the right kind of paper? If you are lucky you may find some around your house. You may find a package of good quality typewriting paper. Perhaps there is some old stationery that is not being used any more. Maybe there is some kind of bookkeeping or office paper that you can get your hands on. Heavy brown wrapping paper is suitable for certain purposes. You may have an old drawing pad which will provide the paper for a book. Filler paper, the kind made for loose-leaf note-books, can be used, although it is often ruled. Construction paper which is used for many different kinds of art projects is excellent for books which need a fairly heavy weight paper. It comes in a variety of colors, and is usually sold in packages of up to a hundred sheets.

If you can't find any decent paper around your house you will have to go out and buy some. Any art supply store or stationery store that carries art materials will have a selection of paper. You will do best to buy a few large single sheets of paper, rather than a pad which you will then have to cut apart.

The single sheets of paper that art and stationery stores carry usually measure about 23 inches by 29 inches. One sheet this size when cut up and folded will make a 32-page book 7 inches by 5½ inches. Two sheets could make a 64-page book. More about this in the next chapter.

Most personal books turn out well if you use a white paper. One of the best is a Strathmore brand, kid finish paper, which is available in most art stores and will cost about forty cents a sheet. This is a very expensive, top quality paper made from rags. There are similar papers which are not made from rags, which are almost as good, and which will cost a great deal less. The term *kid finish* refers to the surface of a paper. Kid finish is just slightly rougher than the surface of the paper on which this book is printed. It is ideal for pencil, or pen-and-ink, or watercolor, or most any writing or drawing instrument you are liable to use.

When you choose a paper feel it and look closely at the surface. Some papers have a very smooth, shiny surface. This would be fine for drawing with pen-and-ink, but not so good for pencil, or pastels, or watercolor. Other papers have a rough, textured surface. Because a pen point has a delicate, sharp tip it will snag and catch on a rough paper. Even a ball point pen—which isn't very good for drawing—won't work well on a coarse paper.

There is a medium-surface paper called *charcoal paper* which is intended for use with charcoal, pastels, or soft pencils. It comes in many handsome colors, has a pleasant feel, and is not too expensive. A 19-inch by 23-inch piece of this kind of paper costs about twenty cents. It is fine for many kinds of books.

There are a great many other kinds of paper. There are watercolor papers, etching papers, rice papers, and so on. Some of them are quite expensive. If you do go shopping for paper, the best thing to do is ask to look at "drawing paper," or "charcoal paper," and then rummage around until you find what you like at a price that you are able to afford.

Another consideration when choosing paper is its weight. Some paper is heavy and stiff. If you intend to fold your paper, anything that is too heavy to fold easily won't do. If you were making a photo album, however, you might want a stiff paper. With a heavy, stiff paper there would be less danger of buckling when you paste in your photographs. In this case you might have to choose a style of binding where no folding was required. Different binding methods are explained in Chapter 4.

Most people take paper for granted. It's just something to write or draw on. But artists, printmakers, people who care about books take it very seriously, and know that it can be a very beautiful material of an extremely varied character. They will pick up a sheet of paper and look at it as carefully as a sculptor examines a block of marble before starting to carve it.

2/ What Size? How Many Pages?

If you have decided on the kind of book you want to make you will probably have some idea about the size it should be. But before you decide the exact size consider what can be economically cut out of the paper you have to work with. If you had a supply of paper that measured 24 inches by 24 inches you would have no waste with a page size that was 12 inches by 12 inches, or 6 inches by 12 inches, and so on.

The number of pages you need will depend on the kind of book you are making and what your ideas are. In general, a small size book should have fewer pages than a large one. For example, a book measuring no more than 3 inches by 4 inches with fifty or sixty pages would be difficult to bind and awkward to handle. The weight of the paper is another consideration. If you are using a very

heavy paper your book will quickly get quite bulky. The ship's log shown above is 6 inches high by 10 inches wide, uses a fairly heavy drawing paper, and has one hundred and twenty pages. This is a big book, using a lot of paper, but it is perfectly manageable, and easy to write and draw in. The book of poems has only thirty-two pages, including the cover. It is 5 inches wide and 7½ inches high.

One of the simplest ways of putting a book together is by cutting out pieces of paper which can be folded in half to make four-page sections. Then these four-page sections can be slipped one inside the other and sewn along the fold. (This is explained in greater detail in Chapter 4.) If you have decided that you are going to bind your book like this you'll need paper cut twice as wide as the individual page. For example, suppose you wanted a 24-page book that was 6 inches by 6 inches. Then you would need six pieces of paper 6 inches by 12 inches.

The drawing below shows one way of cutting up a large sheet of paper so as to get the best use of it.

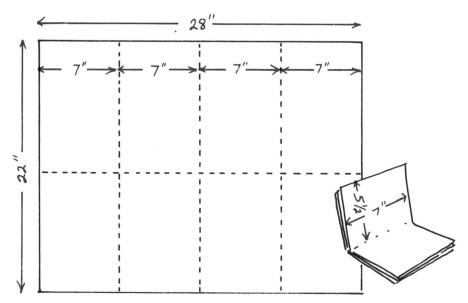

If a sheet of paper 22 by 28 inches was cut up and folded as shown, you would end up with a book of thirty-two pages. Each page would measure 5½ inches wide and 7 inches high.

3 / Cutting and Folding

When you have your paper and know what size your book is to be you can measure and draw the lines along which your paper is to be cut. A yardstick will be very handy if you are working with large sheets of paper.

The cutting is best done with a mat knife or a single-edge razor. (Don't ever try to use a double-edge shaving razor!) Use a straightedge as a guide for your knife or razor and you will get a neat clean cut. A long steel ruler is the ideal straightedge. If you can't find one of these use a piece of plastic or aluminum, or any stiff material with a true edge.

If your paper is heavy or if you are cutting several sheets at one time the blade may not cut all the way through the first time. Make as many passes as necessary, being careful not to let your straightedge slip. It is better to make several, well-controlled passes with your blade rather than one very heavy cut where you have to press down very hard.

Needless to say any sharp knife or razor is dangerous, and particularly so when you are running it along a straightedge. If you are pressing hard and trying to cut swiftly it is quite possible the blade will skip onto the top of the ruler and then right into your finger. So don't press down with all your might. And don't be in a hurry. Slow and easy does it.

If you are working on a good table or a finished floor

be sure to put something underneath your paper. A heavy piece of cardboard or a piece of plywood will protect the surface underneath.

In the event that you can't find a proper knife or razor you'll have to use scissors. Carefully measure and rule the line along which you will cut. Use a large, sharp pair of scissors and take your time. A good pair of scissors will do as neat a job as a knife or razor if you are careful. The cutting will simply take a little more time.

When you fold your pages be careful that the corners overlap perfectly so that your crease will be right down the center. If you are folding really heavy paper you must first *score* it. This means to run a dull blade along the line where the paper will fold. Measure where the fold is to be. Rule a line. Then run your blade against a ruler placed on this line. Any blunt edge can be used—a paper clip, the edge of a coin, or the edge of a spoon will do the trick. The score is made on the inside of the fold. If you don't follow this procedure the fold will be difficult to control and sloppy looking.

8

4/Binding: Stapling and Sewing

The term *binding* is sometimes used to describe the cover of a book. For example, you might refer to a book as having a binding of leather, or being bound in linen. But binding also means the act of attaching many pages to one another to produce a book. For example, if you are stapling pages together as described below you are binding a book.

There are several different ways to bind a book. The two most common ones are explained here.

Stapling You can bind your book in a very simple and effective way if you have the use of a stapler. Cut your individual pages to exactly the same size. Pile them up. Then staple down along one edge. That's all there is to it. The staples may not look very neat and this edge of your book may have a somewhat unfinished look. But this can be easily fixed by pressing on a piece of

cloth adhesive tape over the bound edge. This tape is strong and sticks well. It comes in a roll and can be found in most art or stationery stores. A common brand name is Mystik tape. It comes in various widths and in many beautiful, bright colors. A 2-inch width is best for our purposes. Another way to hide the staples is by attaching a separate cover as explained in Chapter 6.

There are two disadvantages to this kind of binding. One is that the finished book will never open up completely. The staples are pinching it closed along the bound edge. You can't lay the book down on a table and have it stay flat unless you hold it down with your hands. The other difficulty is that there is a limit to how many sheets of paper the stapler will fasten. The heavier the paper the fewer sheets you can use.

If your book is very small (about 3 inches wide) you can make it out of four-page sections and staple the sections together through the fold. This will take care of the two difficulties, but a 3-inch-wide book has very limited uses. (It is a size for pocket memos, tiny pictures, short poems, etc.) There are special staplers which have a very long arm. These will let you staple through the fold of a normal size book. But such staplers are rather hard to find and not worth buying unless you plan to go into the bookmaking business.

Sewing This is a neater and more permanent way to bind a book. It is suitable for a hundred pages or for eight pages. A book that is bound this way is "center-sewn." The drawings on the next page show how it is done.

If you are sewing only a few pages together you can use a plain, heavy, button thread. But if you are binding

SEWING A BOOK TOGETHER

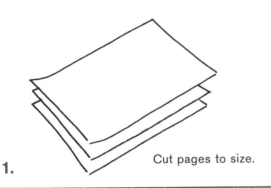

1. Cut pages to size.

2. Fold in half.

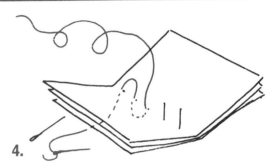

3.

Punch five holes through the fold. The best way to do this is by hammering thin nails through the paper. Use a scrap of wood underneath to protect the top of your work table.

4.

Don't take the nails out until you are ready to run your thread through the holes. This will keep the holes lined up and make the sewing easier.

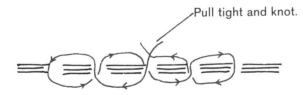

Pull tight and knot.

5.

This is the path of the thread through the holes. If you are making a small, thin book you can get by with three holes instead of five.

6.

Cut off the leftover thread and you have a neat, strong binding.

a rather large book, or making a book that you expect will get hard use or using heavy paper it would be a good idea to use a really heavy, strong thread, doubled up if necessary. I have always used a thin, braided nylon fishing line which is called *squidding line*. It looks nice and is almost unbreakable. Any fisherman is liable to have some. (Three or four feet is enough for several books.) Or you can buy a roll in any sporting goods store. Get the thinnest. (Don't use the glassy-looking monofilament fishing line which is hard to knot.)

When several four-page sections have been sewn together you'll find that the pages which are in the center will tend to project out slightly beyond the outer pages as shown below. This is of no consequence if you are making a book of only twenty or thirty pages. But if your book uses heavy paper and there are many pages you may

The center pages will bulge out if the book is more than twenty or thirty pages thick.

cut off

prefer the edges flush and even. In this case you will have to do a little trimming. Use a metal ruler and a single-edge razor, or a very sharp knife. Press down hard on the ruler so that the paper won't shift. Take your time and make as many passes with the blade as necessary. This is a rather delicate operation and must be done carefully. But when you are through the entire book will have a neat, professional look and you will no doubt decide it was worth the effort.

It is possible to sew together individual pages, as well as four-page sections. However you can't sew along the centerfold—as there is none. What you must do is punch holes *along the edge* and then sew the pages together. The result will be something like the edge stapling already described. The drawings show how this kind of binding is done. A book bound like this is said to be "side-sewn."

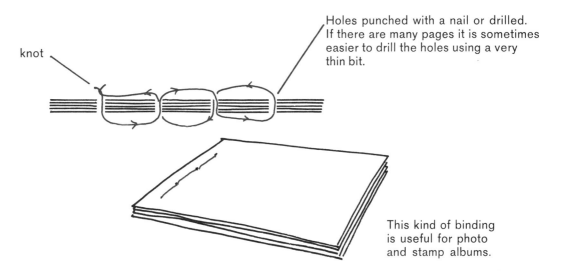

knot

Holes punched with a nail or drilled. If there are many pages it is sometimes easier to drill the holes using a very thin bit.

This kind of binding is useful for photo and stamp albums.

5 / Glueing

There are many times in the making of books when you will want to do some glueing. Here are some methods that will produce a neat, permanent job.

There are many different kinds of glues and pastes to choose from. A white paper paste, or "library paste," is good for most purposes. It is thick, inexpensive, and available in any five-and-ten-cent or stationery store. It is quite easy to make your own paste. A little flour and water is all you need. Put a couple of spoonfuls of flour in a cup or small bowl. Then slowly add water and stir until you get a thick paste.

A white casein glue such as Elmer's is another good glue. It is more expensive than paper paste but most useful when you are pasting down heavy or nonporous materials. If you wanted to paste down a leaf, or some grass, or a lock of hair, a white casein glue would be the kind to use.

Rubber cement is best avoided because it will stain the paper and isn't very permanent. The very strong glues such as the epoxies or Duco cement are not really intended for use with paper.

When you are pasting down a large piece of paper it is sometimes helpful to thin your glue or paste with a little water. This will let you brush it on more easily and evenly. Use a good-sized brush. A 1- or 2-inch wide paint brush is much better than a delicate little watercolor brush with scruffy bristles.

In general it is best to use the least amount of paste that will do the job. When the paste is applied too heavily it will take a long time to dry and will be more likely to cause wrinkles and buckling.

When you have finished your pasting it is important to place some heavy weights on your book. The more the better. This will help avoid wrinkling. Professional bookbinders have special presses and whenever they have done any pasting they put the book in the press and keep it there overnight.

Let's take an example of a pasting job and see just how it should be done. Suppose you were making a book of trees, and you had a photograph of a tree clipped from a magazine that you wanted to include in your book. First, trim the clipping to the size you want. Place it face down on a piece of newspaper. Using a good-sized brush spread the paste on the back of the clipping. Then pick it up and lay it in place in the book. Put a piece of clean paper over the clipping and smooth it down. Rub from the center toward the edges to remove any air bubbles. If any paste squeezes out from under the edges wipe it up with a bit of damp rag. Then close the book and pile as much weight on it as possible. Let it dry for an hour or two or overnight.

6/Covers

Any book will be enormously improved if it has some kind of a cover. The cover doesn't have to be cloth or cardboard or particularly heavy. As long as it has a somewhat different appearance from the inside of the book you can consider it a cover. If, for example, you made a twelve-page book using a different color paper for the outside section you would have a cover of sorts. The different color would seem to "frame" the inside and give it a little more importance.

If you have already made a book and then decide

This cover uses gift wrapping paper. The paper, which is quite flimsy, was pasted down onto some heavy paper. This, in turn, was cut to size and folded in half. Then the cover and inside pages were sewn together through the center fold.

This cover was made by putting a few drops of ink on a sheet of paper then folding the paper over and rubbing it while the ink was still wet. The finished design was then pasted down on cardboard to make the kind of cover described on page 19.

An old marine chart was pasted onto cardboard to make this cover. Road maps, which are similar to marine charts, are easy to come by and are also quite effective when used in this way. The title was clipped out of a magazine and pasted on a piece of colored paper. This in turn was pasted onto the chart.

Two small linoleum blocks were used in a repeated pattern to make this cover. This is an easy way to get some very effective designs.

after it is finished to add a cover you can simply cut a piece of paper as shown below and fasten it permanently in place by pasting the flaps of the cover to the front and back of the book.

This kind of cover is made with flaps which are folded over the front and rear pages and held in place with paste.

A handsome cover can be made by using a piece of paper that has a nice pattern on it. Some of the larger art stores carry decorative, printed papers. Or if you rummage around your house you may be able to find printed papers that you like. How about maps, charts, or wallpaper? You can make your own pattern by pasting down on paper clippings from magazines. You can make all-over patterns quite simply by printing with a cork or rubber eraser. Put a dab of paint on the cork or eraser, then press it down on your paper.

Sometimes the paper you find may be too thin to make a good cover. A road map, for example, is printed on fairly thin paper, and will also have creases from being folded up. In a case like this you would have to paste it down carefully on another sturdier sheet of paper.

Hard Covers A hard cover will make your homemade book look important. It will dress it up as well as give the inside pages some protection. The method for making them shown here is quite simple, but even so you should work slowly and carefully if you want a neat, professional-looking job.

The kind of cardboard you use for the cover is very important. It must be stiff and strong. Shirt cardboard or the cardboard from boxes of store-bought merchandise is usually too thin and flexible. Corrugated board is also to be avoided. Take a look at a regular, hardcover book and notice the stiffness and thickness of the cover. This is what to look for. The cardboard that is used for the backs of large drawing pads is usually suitable and cigar boxes are made of a heavy cardboard that is ideal for our purposes. If all else fails you can buy a heavy cardboard called *chipboard* at any well-supplied art store.

Because cardboard is not a very good-looking material some kind of paper should be pasted down over it. Any decorative paper of the sort mentioned on the previous page can be used.

The other item you need is some cloth tape, such as Mystik tape. This tape has a strong adhesive on one side, is available in many colors, and comes in several widths. A 2-inch roll is best, though you could get by with a 1½-inch width if nothing else is available. Surgical adhesive tape can also be used. And still another possibility is plain cloth. Sailcloth, heavy cotton duck, canvas, or any similar strong, rough material can be used. A white casein glue, like Elmer's, will hold any cloth like this onto the cardboard.

MAKING HARD COVERS

1.

Cut the cardboard to size. You need one piece for the front, another for the back. Usually the covers of a book are slightly larger than the page size.

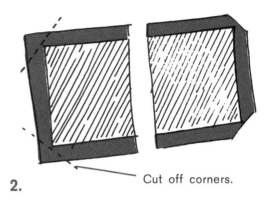

Cut off corners.

2.

Cut your decorative paper ¾ of an inch wider than the cardboard on three sides.

3.

Apply paste generously to the back of the paper, using a good-sized brush.

4.

Place the cardboard on top of the paper. Press down firmly. Fold the extra ¾-inch strip of paper over the edge of the cardboard.

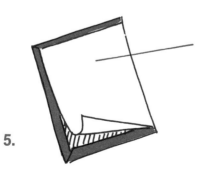

Paste a sheet of white paper over the exposed cardboard.

(Both front and back covers are handled in the same way.)

5.

6.

Leave about a ¾-inch space between the covers. If there are going to be a lot of pages in the book leave more space; if only a few pages, less space. Join the front and back covers together with adhesive cloth tape. If you don't have adhesive cloth tape you can use a strip of any strong cloth such as linen, cotton, or buckram and attach it with paste or a strong glue.

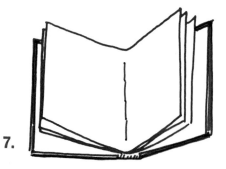

7.

The book is sewn together as described on page 11, only now the thread goes through the tape that is holding the front and back cover together, as well as through the center fold of the inside pages.

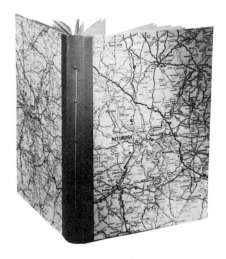

Here is a book with hard covers that was bound using the method just described.

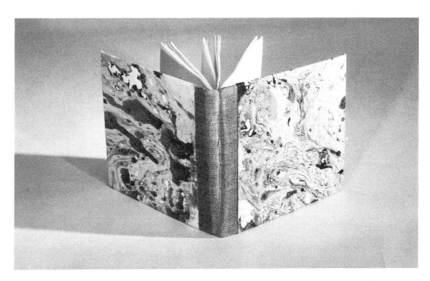

This is a small book with marbleized paper pasted onto cardboard covers. In this book the front and back covers are joined by means of a glued-on strip of linen, instead of adhesive cloth tape.

Marbleized Paper   This is a traditional method of decorating paper. Bookbinders use this kind of paper a great deal. It always looks good. It is very easy to make, requires few materials, and is great fun. Marbleized paper will make a fine cover for a book, or can be used wherever you feel the need for a decorative paper. In fact, you could make an entire book of just marbleized papers—showing different colors and patterns. This is how it is done:

1. Get a shallow tray or pan. It must be big enough to take the size paper you plan to use. Fill it with water.

2. Mix some *oil base* paint with turpentine. Make the paint fairly thin. About a quarter of a teaspoon of paint to a teaspoon of turpentine is a good proportion. You can use any common house paint, or artist's paint—but it must have an oil base.

3. Allow a few drops of the thinned paint to fall into the pan of water. They will float on top and spread out. With a stick spread or swish around the drops of paint until they form a pattern you like. (Don't swish around too much or the paint will all run together.) You can use as many colors as you like. Some very beautiful designs are formed when one color swirls about and mixes with another. If you find that the paint doesn't form into swirls and patterns easily in a way that you like, try using the paint mixed with more or less turpentine. Experiment until you get the proportions that work best for you.

4. The paper should not be submerged in the water. Pick up your paper and lower one end *onto* the water. Then pick up this end, and as you do, let the rest of the paper come into contact with the water. Only one side of the paper touches the water. This is a sort of rolling motion with the entire surface of the paper brought into contact with the paint that is floating on the water. This action sounds much more difficult than it is, and if, in fact, you simply let the paper plop onto the water and then picked it up you would still get good results. One "dip" of the paper onto the water will pick up most of the floating paint. There is rarely any reason to repeat the process. But, sometimes you may decide that another color pattern added to what you already have will be an improvement. In this case you can add some more paint to the water, swish it about and dip the paper a second time.

5. Allow the paint to dry for a few minutes, then place the paper between two sheets of clean paper and put weights on top. This will keep it flat.

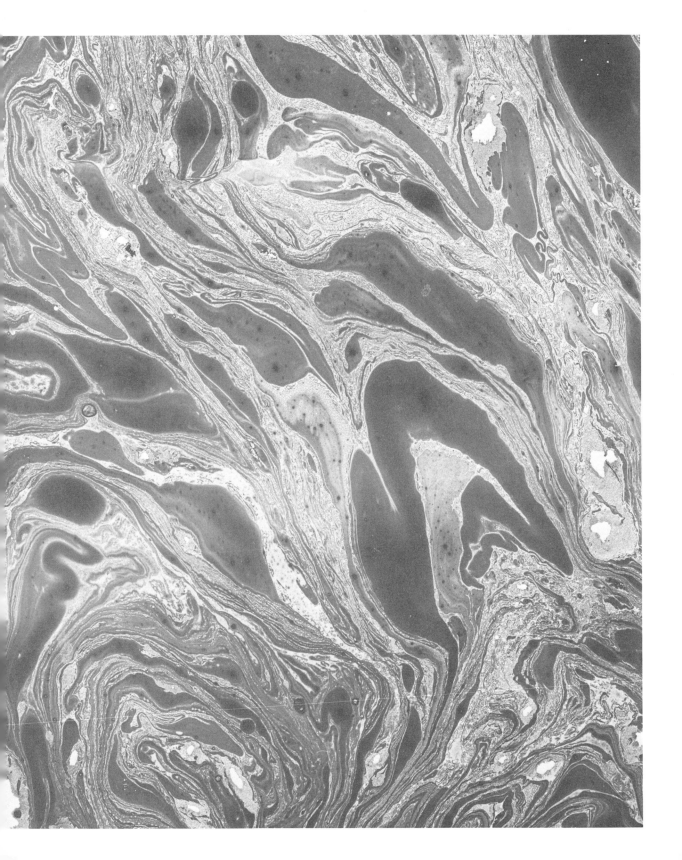

7 / Writing and Printing

Many of the books described in the second half of this book need at least a few written words. They may be a title, or a caption, or a heading, or a note of explanation. In the case of a diary or story book there may be nothing but writing in the book. So this matter is worth a little thought.

When your book is mostly written you can simply use your normal handwriting, or printing, being as careful and neat as possible. But if you want to get fancy you can buy a chisel-pointed pen and the special ink made for it at an art supply store (they will cost three or four dollars) and do the sort of writing shown here. This is a rather slow way to write, but many people think the results are worth it. It is not difficult if you have an average handwriting because the pen point does most of the

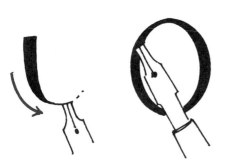

Writing and Printing

Writing and Printing

Writing and Printing

ABCD

Practice

FG

a bcdefghijklm
nopqrstuvwxyz.

work for you. The elegant, thick-thin line is produced naturally by the changing angle of the pen point as it moves over the paper in different directions. It will be helpful if you rule thin pencil lines as guides—unless you are in the habit of writing in straight lines.

This chisel-edge style of writing is very similar to that used in the days before the printed book was invented. For thousands of years all books were handwritten and scribes used quill pens (which had a chisel point) to produce beautiful pages, like the one illustrated on page 28.

Sometimes a typewriter is useful—if you have one and know how to use it. You can't very well put your whole book in the typewriter, but you can type on single pieces of paper and then paste them in your book. If the paper on which you type is carefully cut to the proper size and then neatly pasted on the page it can look quite attractive.

When it comes to large-size printing—for titles or chapter headings, or anything much larger than the normal handwriting size—you will probably want to be a little more particular. With a good deal of practice you might learn to produce very neat lettering like the kind shown below. But it isn't too easy. What many people do

is use a very loose, almost cartoon-style of lettering. Unevenness, variations in size and style, and awkward letters are intentional. You can get quite effective results even if you hate the idea of lettering and are convinced you can't do it! Experiment a little and see if you can't find your own personal style.

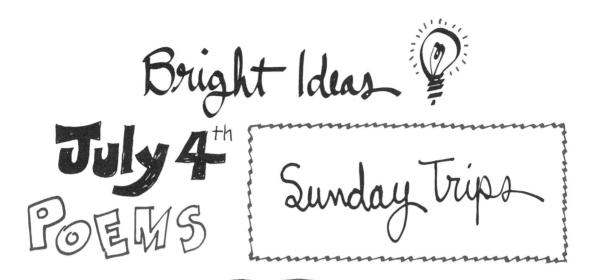

There are a number of ways in which a plain, handwritten page can be dressed up. One of the simplest and most effective is to use decorative initial letters. (In a book or manuscript, the first letter of a chapter, a division of a chapter or a verse is referred to as the initial letter.) The initial letter was often a very elaborate decoration in the first printed books and in handwritten manuscripts. These handwritten manuscripts were most often religious or prayer books of one sort or another and they were usually made for royalty or the extremely wealthy. The scribes and artists who made them took enormous pains and produced very rich decorations and illustrations. Sometimes the initial letters were built up into

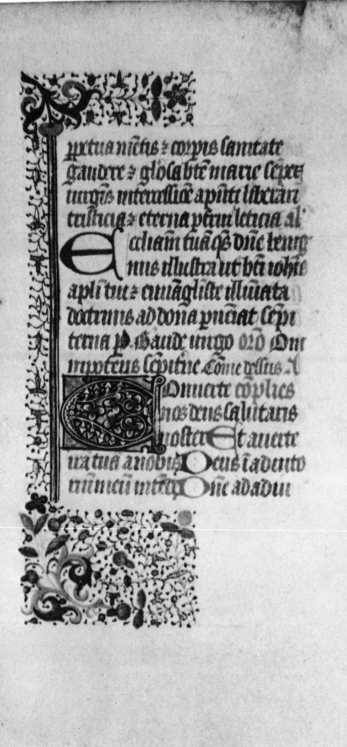

ptua nictis ⁊ corpis sanitate
gaudere ⁊ glosa bte marie se ppe-
turgis intercessiõe a psti liberari
tristicia ⁊ eterna pfrui leticia al'
ecliam tuã qs dñe benig
nius illustra ut bti iohie
apli tui ⁊ euãgliste illuiata
doctrinis ad dona pueniat sepi
terna p. Gaude uirgo oro Oñi
mi pteius seruitie Cõme uersus. A
Onuerte coplices
nos deus salutaris
noster Et auerte
ira tua a nobis Deus ia deuto
riu meũ intẽq Dñe ad adui

miniature paintings of great beauty and enormous detail.

There are other decorative devices—aside from drawings, pasted-in material, initial letters—which can make a book with a lot of writing a little more lively and easier to read. Something as simple as a line of dots in colored ink, or a few stars or curlicues can be used. At times a ruled line or a word in color will be a big help.

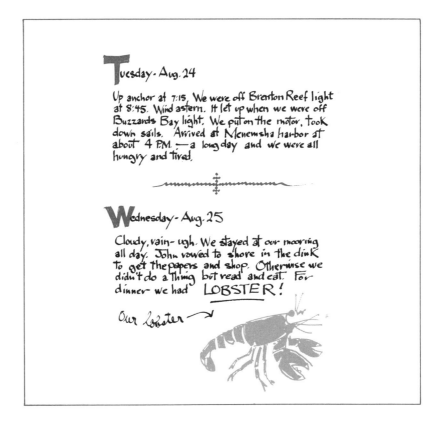

This illustration is from a book that was written by hand in Latin in the early 1400s. The initial letters and elaborate, delicate curlicues and floral decorations make for an elegant and quite beautiful page.

Here is the cover of a sailboat's logbook, and some of the inside pages. As you can see this travel journal has had a lot of hard usage during a long summer of sailing and cruising.

part two BOOKS YOU CAN MAKE

So far we have explained the various methods of putting together the homemade book. Now we can go on to discuss the *content* of the book. The following pages consider different kinds of books, what you can do with them, and what possibilities you have to choose from.

Travel Journals

A travel journal is a record of a trip, a vacation, or a summer's adventures. It is a kind of diary. It is a way to keep a record of where you've been and what happened along the way. You can collect and paste in all sorts of souvenir material. Picture postcards, maps, menus, snapshots, printed material of all kinds can be included.

For many years I have kept a sort of journal—which is actually a ship's log. I call it "The Log of the *Phoebe,*" (*Phoebe* being the name of my boat). I make up a fresh log every year. I keep it on the boat, and whenever I go out for a sail I try to make some kind of notation in the log. It might be very simple, like: "August 15th—bright, clear day. Light SW winds. Liz and John were aboard—and ate a whole box of Fig Newtons! Sailed around Sheffield Island. Left 2 P.M.—returned at 6."

When friends come out for a sail with me I give them the log and ask them to write something in it or draw a picture in it. Sometimes, if there was a lot of interesting activity, I'll take the log home with me after a sail and write a fairly detailed account of what happened, complete with diagrams, sketches, and comments.

Every now and then I go off on my boat for a cruise. It may be only for a weekend, or it may be for two or three weeks. But I find that the trip is more fun when I am keeping a log. And it is also fun years later when I look back over the log and can recall all the adventures and misadventures and good times.

During a cruise, when the day's sail is over and the boat is at a dock or at anchor someone will always grab the logbook and describe what happened during the day— the weather, what we saw, what we talked about, had for lunch, and so on. If we go ashore we'll sometimes bring back a souvenir of some kind which can be pasted in the log. In one of my logs there is a big lock of hair pasted on one page to celebrate a haircut. On another page there is the label from a can of mushroom salad that was particularly tasty. And the log is filled with little sketches, small watercolor paintings, maps, clippings from magazines, corny poetry, assorted nonsense, as well as a more or less serious account of what happened every day.

The ship's logs that I make up for my own use are center-sewn, use a good quality rag paper, and measure 6¼ inches high and 10 inches wide. This size can be cut out of a large sheet of paper without too much waste. It is also convenient to use. It gives me plenty of room to write. It is a pleasant size for sketching and yet it is small enough to be packed away easily. Because the log is sewn along the centerfold it opens up easily, and stays open

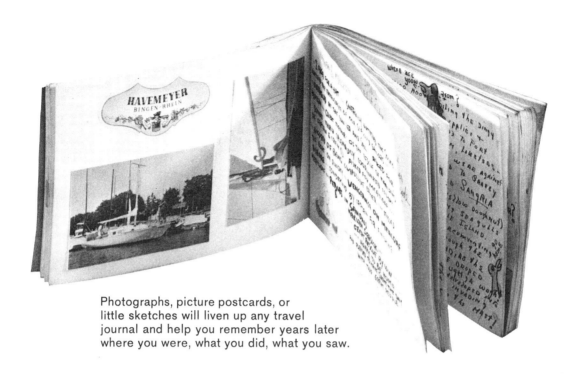

Photographs, picture postcards, or little sketches will liven up any travel journal and help you remember years later where you were, what you did, what you saw.

reasonably well while I am working on it. (This would not be the case with a tall, thin book, regardless of how it was bound.)

You don't have to go off on a cruise to keep a ship's log—or travel journal. You can keep a journal on a weekend camping trip, a fishing trip, an afternoon ride through the countryside, as well as a long vacation trip somewhere.

Photographs are a great addition to a journal. If you have a Polaroid camera you can take your pictures and then immediately paste them in the appropriate places. If you have the usual camera where you have to send away the film to be developed, leave room for the finished prints.

If you make your own travel journal you may choose a page size and style of binding altogether different from the kinds used for the ship's log. There is no correct or ideal way of doing it. It is up to you. You might want a very small journal that can be tucked into a pocket or a backpack. You might want something quite large. The only thing that is important is that you use a good grade of paper, as discussed in the first chapter. It is quite likely that your journal will be knocked about a bit and it's no fun to have pages rip in a breeze, or dissolve if you are caught in a sudden thunder shower.

Diaries

A diary is a personal record of day-to-day events, and it is just like a travel journal. But it is kept up all the time, not just on special occasions.

Many people start diaries and keep them up for a short period of time. Then they lose interest and the diary ends up in the back of a bureau drawer or in a dark corner of a book case. Probably the best way to keep a diary going is to devote just brief notes to the normal, daily activities, and devote most of the space to the things that are special and that you have some thoughts about. When a diary has your ideas, opinions, and reactions it will be a good deal more interesting than a simple factual account of the day's activities.

In any case, it is a good idea to make at least some note in your diary every day—even if it is to write in only the day and date of the week.

Your diary can be whatever size you think convenient. But probably you won't want it to be too big. After all a diary is a personal thing. You may want it small so that you can tuck it away somewhere where everybody isn't going to read it. A reasonable size is 6 inches by 6 inches, but if your handwriting is small you might want a smaller size.

The number of pages in the diary will be decided to some extent by the style of binding and the kind of paper you are using. But even if you intend to write a great deal you don't need an awkwardly thick book. After all, several slim volumes will hold as much as one fat one.

Most diaries look best with some sort of cover, and you might consider attaching two short pieces of ribbon so that the covers can be tied closed. This won't lock up your diary, but it will hint that this volume is private and not for curious eyes.

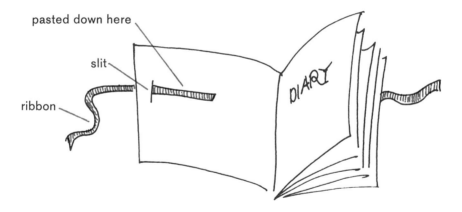

pasted down here

slit

ribbon

DIARY

If you are going to have ribbons to tie up your diary it is best to use a fairly heavy paper for the cover or else use a hard cover. The ribbon goes through a slit in the cover and is pasted down on the inside.

Flip Books

A flip book is a small book with pictures that very gradually change from one page to the next. When you let the pages riffle by under your thumb the pictures blend into one another and there is the illusion of motion. It is very much like looking at a movie with no sound. In the illustration below, if the drawings of the bird were on separate pages and you let these pages rapidly flip over, the bird would seem to flap its wings.

Flip books are small in size—but as thick as you can conveniently make them. The one thing that is extremely important is getting the edges of the pages lined up evenly. The pages must slip out from under your thumb in a steady sequence without pauses or jerks. It doesn't matter if the other three edges of a flip book are ragged or don't quite line up. It's the "thumb edge" that counts.

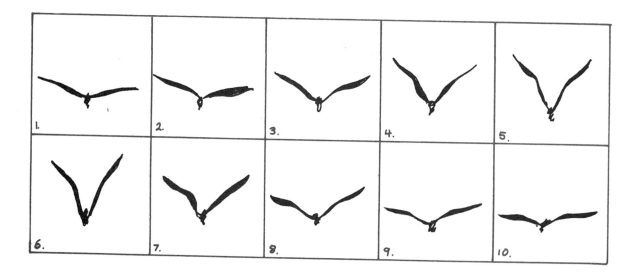

A flip book will usually have 40 or 50 leaves (or 80 or 100 pages, if you count both sides of the paper) so it will be too thick for the average staple machine. You'll find that the simplest way to bind it is to punch two or three holes with a thin nail and then sew the book together. Another similar method is to place the pages on a board and drill two holes. Then fasten the pages together with nuts and bolts. This may look a little clumsy but it works well. Before you make any holes, however, tap the "thumb edge" on a flat surface to make sure that this edge is perfectly even.

If, despite all your efforts, you find that your "thumb edge" is not smooth and even when the book is bound, you have no choice but to trim this edge with a knife (as described in Chapter 4). Use a steel ruler or metal edge as a guide and be sure your knife is razor sharp—or use a single-edge razor.

If you find that you can't get the pages of your flip book to riffle out smoothly and evenly from under your

thumb you'll have to do the following: Take the binding apart. Arrange the pages so that they are slightly staggered as shown in the margin. Then punch new holes and bind up the book again maintaining this arrangement. You'll find that the flipping will go much more smoothly.

When you make a flip book you are faced with the task of drawing as many pictures as there are pages. So don't attempt a scene with many complicated elements. This would be tedious and take a great deal of time. Keep it simple. Stick figures are perfectly all right. Flat abstract shapes can be used. Simple subjects like a bird, a tree, a face, a cloud can be the basis for very interesting sequences. Don't worry if you can't draw well. What is most interesting about flip books is the motion and the ideas—not the drawing skill.

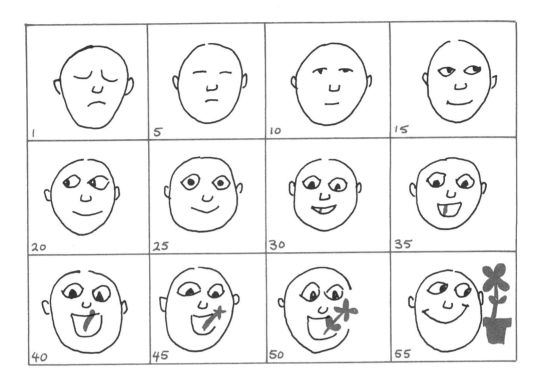

Flip books are fascinating not only because of the way you can get things to move, but because of the way you can produce changes. An automobile can turn into a flower. A bird can flap its wings, get smaller and gradually disappear, replaced by a telephone. A seed can grow and become a flower. The possibilities are endless.

One of the problems you'll meet with as you work on a flip book is placing a picture on one page in proper relationship to the one immediately before it. The easiest way to handle this is to do your drawing with a pencil and press down hard. The pencil will leave an impression on the page under the one you are working on. You can use this impression as a guide for your next drawing.

Photo Albums

With photo albums, as with all the books described on these pages, you have a big choice of sizes and styles. This is one of the great satisfactions in making your own books. You can make something which is entirely your own. You might want a square-shaped album, or one with a yellow cover, or an album of a special size. If you go to a store you'll find only conventional albums, and the nice ones are sure to be quite expensive. If you make your own album it may not be quite as slick looking as the store-bought variety, but you'll know that no one else in the world will have one exactly like it!

When you plan your photo album refer to the size of the prints you are going to mount. How many prints do you want on each page? Will you need room for captions? If you have photographs of particular subjects or at different times, or different places, you may want to make separate, smaller albums. For example, you could have an album of portraits, or landscapes, or pictures taken during one summer, and so on.

One of the most interesting projects is to make a picture story of some sort and devote an entire little album to it. The album shown above is like this. It describes one day in the life of a baby. There is only one print with a short caption on each page. The position of each picture was decided before binding. Then the captions were typed, the pages sewn together, and the prints pasted in place. This particular album is 7 inches by 7 inches.

The picture story album has many possibilities. You might try making up a story and illustrating it with photographs. Or you might want to do a picture essay on some theme you are particularly interested in. You could do one on pollution, traffic congestion, a school visit somewhere, or a day's outing. There are many possibilities.

There are many different opinions about how a photograph should be fastened on an album page. But the simplest way is to use just a small dab of glue on each corner of the print. A white casein glue such as Elmer's will hold securely. Rubber cement is not permanent and will stain the print.

The kind of paper you use in an album will have a lot to do with the way it looks. If you use a thin drawing or writing paper the album will look flimsy and delicate. When you paste anything on thin paper like this you can't help but get unsightly wrinkling and buckling. When there is going to be a lot of pasting you need a really heavy paper. Most stationery stores have "filler" paper which is intended for use in commercial photo albums. You can use this, or you can get charcoal paper from an art store. This comes in many attractive, soft colors and is fairly heavy. It is a good choice for albums. You can also use construction paper. The paper you use is important so choose it with care. Chapter 1 in the first part of this book discusses paper in some detail; binding methods are described in Chapter 4; and a somewhat more elaborate binding method that is excellent for all kinds of albums is described on page 45.

Stamp Albums

A stamp album, like a photo album, should be carefully planned before you finally decide on size and style. You should determine how much room you need on a page, what you want to include, how much room to leave for future acquisitions, and so on. Perhaps you want to have several small albums—one for United States stamps, one for colonials, one for commemoratives, or whatever.

There is one thing to bear in mind when you are making a stamp album. If you are an active collector your collection will be always changing. You will be getting

Here you can see how the covers and pages are held firmly in place, and yet the cover is free to open up wide.

new stamps, trading, shifting things about. So you will want to be able to add or remove pages or change their position. If your album is sewn down the centerfold you can't remove only one leaf, because this binding style requires four-page sections. Therefore it is best to use some kind of side-sewn binding where each leaf is separate. With this kind of binding you can simply untie or cut the thread or string holding the pages together, add or remove pages, then tie or sew it all up again.

If you aren't going to add or remove pages and you want a heavy board cover you can use a binding like the kind shown opposite. This not only looks nice but provides good protection for your stamps. This binding is also good for photo albums.

HARDCOVER BINDING FOR ALBUMS

1.

Cut the cardboard to size, then cut a strip off one side about ¾ of an inch wide. (The steps shown here must be done twice—to get front and back covers.)

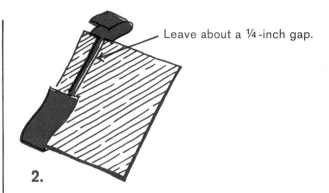

Leave about a ¼-inch gap.

2.

Use an adhesive cloth tape such as Mystik brand tape to join the cover to the strip.

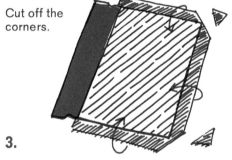

Cut off the corners.

3.

Paste a decorative paper of some sort over what will be the outside of the cover. This paper should be about ¾ of an inch wider than the cardboard on three sides. These extra edges are folded over and pasted down.

4.

Another sheet of paper is pasted down over the exposed cardboard on the inside of the cover.

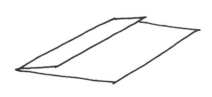

5.

Cut out the pages for your album. Because the material that will be pasted in will make the album fairly bulky it is a good idea to make your pages an inch wider than needed. Then this extra inch can be folded over as shown. This extra layer of paper along the bound edge will keep the album from bulging as you paste in stamps and other material.

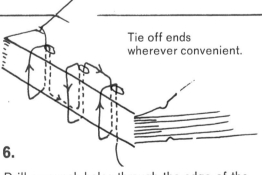

Tie off ends wherever convenient.

6.

Drill or punch holes through the edge of the cover and through the inside pages. The sewing method shown here puts loops of thread over the outside edges of the album, which make for a quite strong fastening.

Scrapbooks

A scrapbook is just like a stamp or photo album. The only difference is the sort of thing you put in it—which can be just about anything! Many people use a scrapbook to keep clippings about some subject in which they are particularly interested. Suppose you were a basketball fan and followed the career of one special player. A scrapbook would be a good way to keep and collect news stories about this person. Or maybe you are interested in sailboats, or gorillas, or politics in New Zealand, or antique clocks, or carpentry projects, or most anything else—a scrapbook is a fine way to keep together all the information you can gather on your special subject.

As with the other albums already mentioned, the heavier the paper the better, and after you've done your pasting it is a good idea to weight down the book with as much weight as possible.

Japanese Style Books

In the Far East there are styles of bookbinding which are quite different from the western styles. The Japanese book illustrated opposite shows one of these. It is put

This book was printed in Japan using age-old techniques and binding methods. It is quite an elaborate production requiring a great deal of patience and skill. Some of the illustrations are printed with as many as twelve different colors.

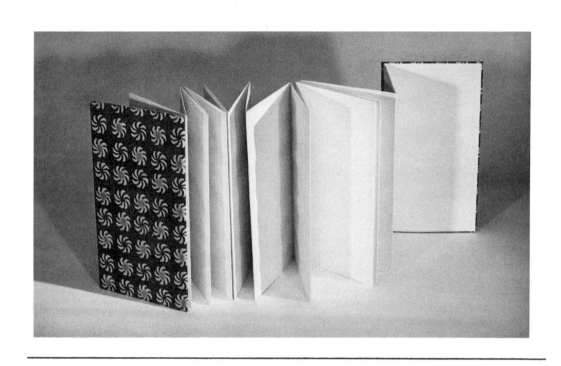

together without sewing or stapling. It can be held in the hand like the books we are familiar with, and the pages can be turned a page at a time. But it also can be un-folded like an accordion. In fact, commercial printers and binders refer to this kind of folding as "accordion folding."

The book on page 47 is printed in many colors from wood blocks. Printing of this sort is done on thin, delicate rice paper. This is fragile paper which is not strong enough to be bound into a book. Therefore these thin papers are glued onto a heavier sheet of paper, which is then folded and pasted to the covers. This book tells a story by means of the pictures and short captions. The story is continued on the reverse side.

A book of this sort is easy to put together and fun to experiment with. It lends itself to all sorts of uses. It can be used for keeping a diary or journal. It can be a sketchbook, album, storybook, or in fact, just about anything.

You don't need one very long piece of paper for this kind of book. Though, if you could get your hands on a

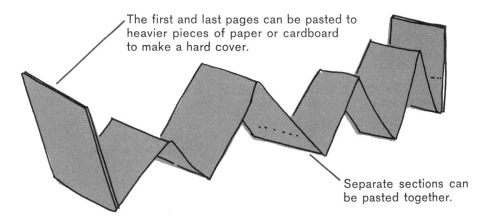

The first and last pages can be pasted to heavier pieces of paper or cardboard to make a hard cover.

Separate sections can be pasted together.

roll of paper such as kitchen shelving paper, or brown wrapping paper you would have a suitable material. What you can do is paste together several pieces of paper to get a long strip, and then fold this.

A sturdy cover of some sort, glued to the ends of the folded pages, will give the book a much more finished look and will also give the inside some protection.

Scrolls

This is another type of "book" that is rather uncommon today. It is a little like the Japanese style book in that it uses a long strip of paper. But here the strip is rolled rather than folded. Scrolls are often quite long, because a great length of paper can be rolled up without getting awkward or clumsy to handle.

A scroll can be used for written text as well as drawing or painting. Jewish religious services include the use of a Torah which is simply a long scroll on which the Old Testament is written. The material used is sheepskin, rather than paper. The individual sections of parchment are sewn together into a very long strip and rolled up on thick wooden rods.

If you decide to make a scroll see if you can find something like two pieces of broomstick handle to roll it up on. These will keep the scroll from getting accidentally damaged or crushed, and will let you handle it with greater

This scroll is attached at either end to short pieces of wood rod. The scroll tells a little story about an imaginary prehistoric animal.

ease. Scrolls have text or illustration on only one side of the paper.

To make a scroll you need a long strip of paper, just as you would for a folded Japanese style book. You might find it simpler to work on a scroll before it is rolled up and attached to the rods because now it will lie flat. But you'll probably find it is more fun to unroll a bit at a time, work on a section, then "roll on" to the next section.

A scroll is a kind of book, as is an accordion-folded Japanese book. So whatever you do with a regular book you can do with a scroll . . . with the exception of pasting on photographs or clippings. Because of the rolling and unrolling of the paper, most pasted material will have a tendency to wrinkle and eventually come loose and would also make the rolling more difficult. If you are doing a lot of writing on a scroll you might find it convenient to divide it up into "pages." A simple, vertical ruled line will accomplish this.

Scrolls are often used for proclamations, formal awards, and presentations. You'll find that a fancy, ornate scroll will make a fine present for someone. Do some very elaborate lettering; paste on ribbons and old stamps; draw a lot of fancy curlicues, stars, and ruled borders. Then spatter on some tea or coffee to give the paper a parchmentlike look. Then write some very formal and stuffy and not necessarily serious message like the ones below. And finally tie up the finished scroll with a ribbon.

Comic Books

At first thought a comic book may seem like a very ambitious undertaking requiring great drawing skill. Some comic books are indeed like this, but not all. There are some which make use of the most simple elements which anybody can draw. Characters and settings like the ones shown below are examples of this sort of thing.

What is interesting with this kind of comic book is the situations, characters, and dialogue you make up—not the artistry of the drawing.

If you decide to try to make a comic book don't spend too much time worrying about how the entire story is going to work out. Just pick a character or two and get started! Let the plot work itself out as you go along. You'll find that ideas will come to you once you've begun. Don't worry if your story wanders and characters appear and disappear in unexplainable ways. In fact, you can have a fine time making a comic book even if your story makes absolutely no sense at all!

Most comic books consist of a series of panels or square frames in which the action takes place. Choose a panel size which seems appropriate for the kind of action you will be making up and the amount of dialogue you will use. A three- or four-inch square is a convenient size. Use a page size which will comfortably hold as many panels as you want per page. If your book is on the small side with two panels per page—or even one per page—you will increase the suspense of your story. The reader won't be able to glance down at the last panel on the page to see where the action is leading.

Give your comic book a cover of some kind, and you might want to make up a very bright and lurid design for it.

Nonsense Books

Any book which isn't very serious or doesn't make much sense can be called a "nonsense book." There are limitless subjects, infinite possibilities, and these books are great fun to make. Here are a few sample titles which will give you some idea of what this kind of book can be like: *The Tattoo Artist's Handbook, How to Build a Dirigible, The Story of My Lion Hunting Expedition in Kenya, How I Built the George Washington Bridge, My Friends and*

Enemies, How I Made My First Million Dollars, Different Careers I Have Had, How to Appear Intelligent.

This sort of book is usually most interesting if it has some illustrations, though this doesn't mean that you have to be able to draw well. Often the most simple or crude drawing will suit your purpose. And in many cases you can use clippings from magazines or newspapers. Almost any page size or binding style can be used.

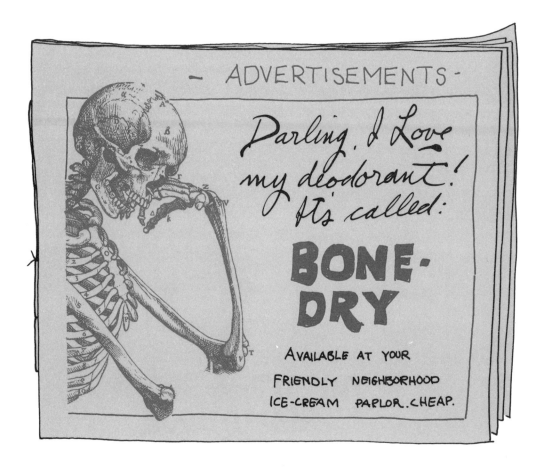

Sketchbooks

These are simply books with blank pages, and they are made in any of the different ways already described. The size is up to you and should suit the purpose to which the book will be put. If you go for hikes or trips and like to make brief little drawings or watercolors you will want a small book which can be easily carried. If you are going to use watercolor or wash make sure that the paper you use is suitable.

If you intend to work large you may not want a sketchbook at all. A few sheets of good quality paper carried in a portfolio might be much more practical. The

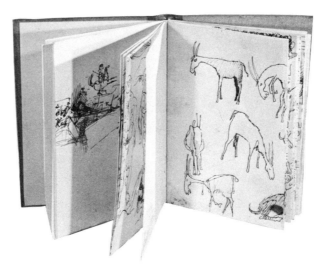

This sketchbook is bound with hard covers. The hard backing can be useful when you are sketching but isn't really essential.

drawings below show how you can make a simple portfolio. Use a *heavy* cardboard (not corrugated board!), and
this will not only protect the paper better, but will serve as
a sort of drawing board on which you can work.

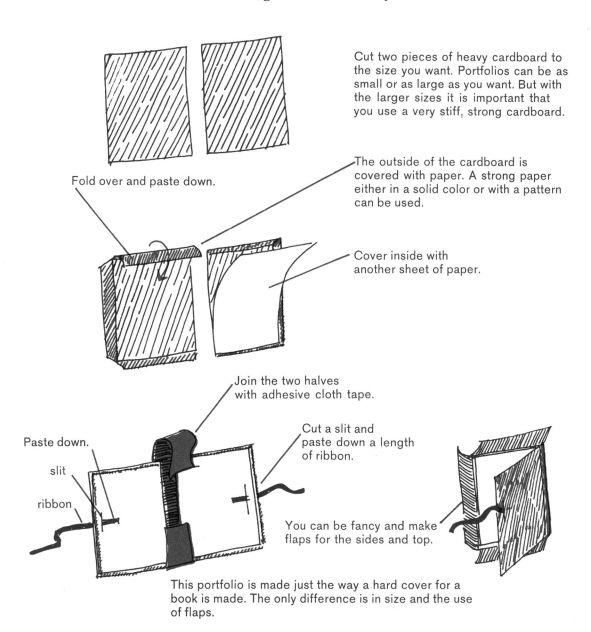

Cut two pieces of heavy cardboard to
the size you want. Portfolios can be as
small or as large as you want. But with
the larger sizes it is important that
you use a very stiff, strong cardboard.

Fold over and paste down.

The outside of the cardboard is
covered with paper. A strong paper
either in a solid color or with a pattern
can be used.

Cover inside with
another sheet of paper.

Join the two halves
with adhesive cloth tape.

Cut a slit and
paste down a length
of ribbon.

Paste down.

slit

ribbon

You can be fancy and make
flaps for the sides and top.

This portfolio is made just the way a hard cover for a
book is made. The only difference is in size and the use
of flaps.

A Book of Rubbings

A rubbing is produced by taking a piece of paper, placing it over a surface which has a definite texture, then rubbing the paper with a pencil or marking crayon. The texture of the surface under the paper will appear on the paper. You've probably tried this with a coin at one time or another. A piece of thin paper is placed over a coin and then the paper is rubbed with a pencil. It is essential that the paper be held down firmly over the coin so that it won't slip while you rub.

There are all sorts of things that lend themselves to rubbing. One of the most popular are old tombstones, and there are people who make a hobby of wandering from one graveyard to another looking for interesting carvings and designs. The problem with tombstone rubbings—which can be very beautiful—is that they are often too large for a book, unless you make a really large book. What you might do is use just details of tombstones.

But there are many other objects which will make good rubbings. How about a fish? (Be sure it's well frozen or you won't have a firm surface to work with.) You might try a series of rubbings to show varieties of bark on trees. How about leaves?

It can be great fun to wander about searching for interesting patterns and textures. You might find subjects in unexpected places . . . perhaps the carving on an

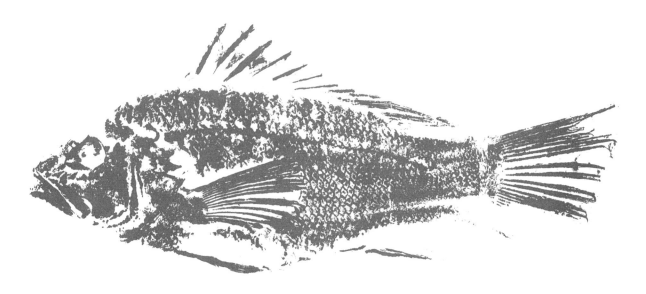

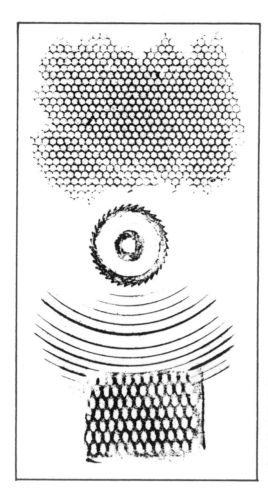

Rubbings from four different objects have been combined here on one sheet of paper. The rubbing on top is from the grill on the back of a radio, below that a gear, then the ridges on a phonograph turntable, and, on the bottom, a cheese grater.

old school desk, the pattern of a metal grill, the embossing on a tin candybox lid, an unusual grain on a rock or piece of driftwood. There are possibilities everywhere.

An ordinary soft pencil will work all right with a coin. But for larger subjects you will do better to use some kind of wax crayon. There are special crayons made for rubbing and you may be able to find one in a well-provisioned art store. These crayons are rectangular in shape, so that you have a wide, straight edge to rub with. The common children's wax crayon is not too good because it doesn't

64

Willow trees were often used on tombstones made in the eighteenth century. ▶

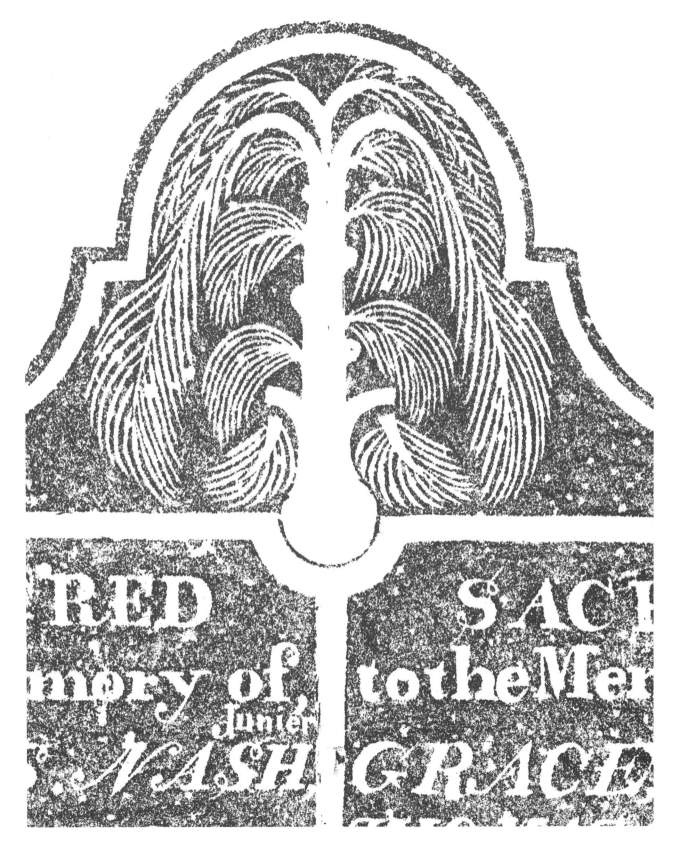

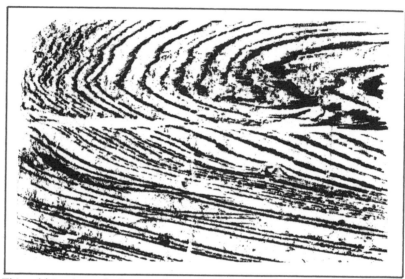

This rubbing is made from a piece of old driftwood.

rub evenly. Pastels and charcoal are also unsatisfactory because they are soft and will smudge easily. Art stores carry a kind of square crayon called a lithographic crayon which will work well, and you can also use the large sticks of lead or graphite (the kind used in pencils) which are made for sketching.

Experiment with different kinds of paper. This too is important. You need a paper that is thin and light, but still reasonably strong. The ideal paper is Japanese rice paper.

When you have a collection of rubbings, cut the paper to the size you want, then bind them together. Because you will have individual pages you will have to sew or staple along the edge. You can paste one of your rubbings on a piece of heavy paper or cardboard and use that for a cover.

Experimental Books

There are many odd and offbeat ways of making books which can be fun to try. And sometimes one of these ways will fit in with something you are doing and help to explain or dramatize an idea.

The drawings below show some of the possibilities, and you may be able to think of some others yourself.

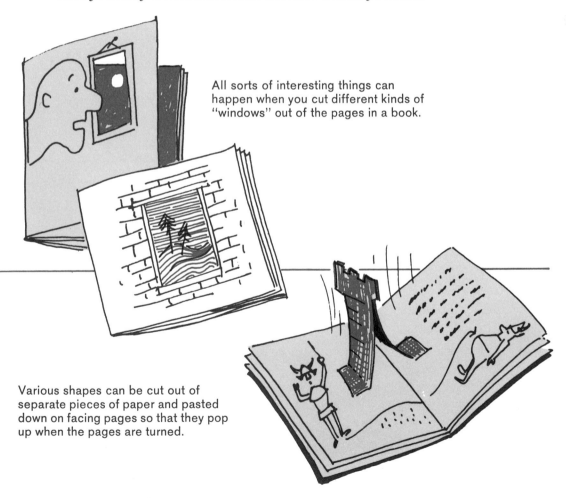

All sorts of interesting things can happen when you cut different kinds of "windows" out of the pages in a book.

Various shapes can be cut out of separate pieces of paper and pasted down on facing pages so that they pop up when the pages are turned.

You can make a "double book" with two front covers and two sets of inside pages. This will let you put together all sorts of unlikely creatures or events. You might, for example, have the head and shoulders of a lion and the rear end of an alligator, or race car, or butterfly.

A small book with blank pages and an ink pad are all you need to make a thumbprint book. Keep the book and pad handy and every time you meet a friend get his thumbprint and autograph in your book. This is an utterly useless project well worth doing.

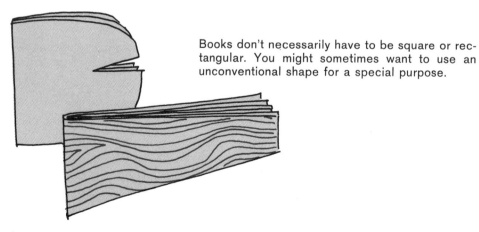

Books don't necessarily have to be square or rectangular. You might sometimes want to use an unconventional shape for a special purpose.

Books of clippings like the one above are similar to scrapbooks—but with one major difference. Instead of pasting the clippings onto a blank page the clipping itself is cut to page size and then sewn or stapled into book form. The clipping is the page itself. All kinds of pictorial material can be used—maps, wallpaper, magazine and advertising clippings, and, in fact, whatever printed material that appeals to you. This kind of book is interesting as an adventure in contrasts and relationships. The combinations of colors and patterns or of different subjects can produce a picture book that is fun to assemble and then thumb through. This sort of book will work best if it is kept on the small side. Something like 5 inches by 5 inches is a good size. Some of the clippings will have on their backs all kinds of printing you didn't choose. You can either ignore this material, or, if you are ambitious and have a good deal of patience—and paste—you can paste the clipped material back to back to form a single page. If you do any photography and can make enlargements you can assemble the finished prints in a manner similar to the one shown above. Four by 5-inch enlargements can be easily side-sewn into book form. This is a practical and convenient way to keep and show your photographs.

A Japanese-type book can be made so that it fits neatly into a small box. This is an unusual and dramatic type of "binding." You take off the cover of the box and the book will pop out, much like a jack-in-the-box. If you can't find a box of the right size you can make one yourself. Paste decorative paper over the assembled box and you'll have something quite handsome.

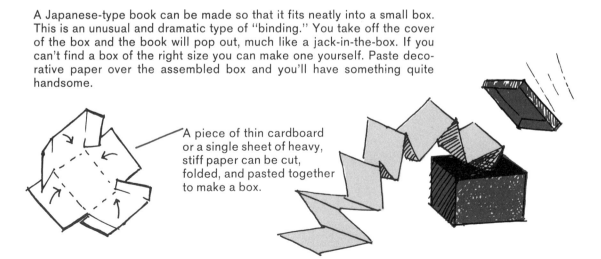

A piece of thin cardboard or a single sheet of heavy, stiff paper can be cut, folded, and pasted together to make a box.

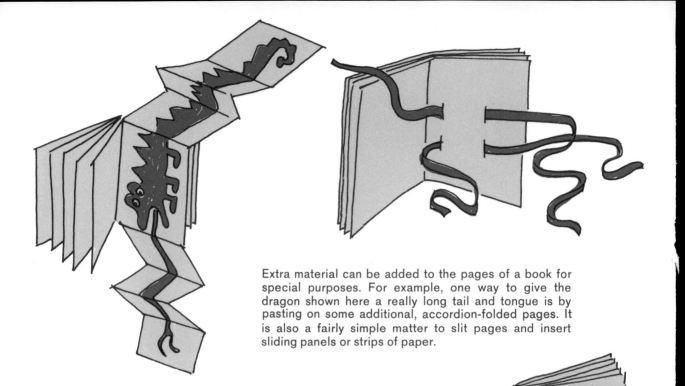

Extra material can be added to the pages of a book for special purposes. For example, one way to give the dragon shown here a really long tail and tongue is by pasting on some additional, accordion-folded pages. It is also a fairly simple matter to slit pages and insert sliding panels or strips of paper.

There is much art which lends itself to use in books. For example, you may have many small drawings, watercolors, or prints which you have collected and which can be assembled into book form. If the dimensions are not too dissimiliar they can be trimmed to one common size and bound together. Or else you can use a book with blank pages, like a sketchbook, and fill it with drawings and sketches based on a single theme. For example, you could make a book of trees, or insects, hats, spacecraft, moustaches, inventions, ideas for impossible and fantastic machines (gumball-chewing devices, haircutting machines, steam engine airplanes), flowers, architectural details, and so on. There are infinite possibilities for books which make use of various art techniques.

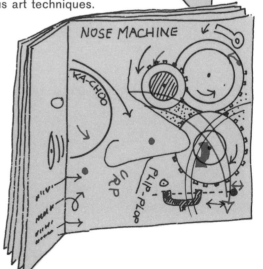

70

Why not go into the publishing business? If you can make linoleum cuts, or stencils, or etchings, or silk-screen prints, or woodcuts, or have the use of even the simplest kind of toy printing press you can produce "limited edition" books! The book shown above is an example of this kind of book. It is made up of a half-dozen etchings accompanied by a few, brief, handwritten poems. Each etching is printed on a piece of paper 15 inches by 8 inches, which is then folded in half to make four pages. There is also a title page. Etching is a slow and laborious way of printing so this book is printed in a very limited edition of six copies! The book illustrated below uses linoleum cuts which are easy to make and can be printed fairly speedily. So a few copies could be printed without too

much effort. Books of this sort have been made by many amateurs interested in printing and in the graphic arts. Some of them, by well known artists and skilled printers, are greatly valued by collectors and are sold for a good deal of money. This kind of book can be simple, small, unpretentious, yet great fun to put together and makes a fine present.

The two books shown on this page depend on their illustrations for their main interest. But there are many books of this sort printed on small printing presses which contain only a brief printed text of some sort, and no pictures at all. If the printing is done with taste and care and the binding carefully made the results are often quite beautiful.

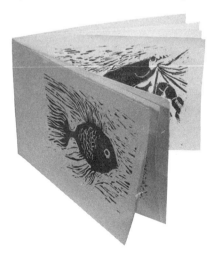

ABOUT HARVEY WEISS

Harvey Weiss is a sculptor whose work is in many museums and private collections. He has done a number of other things, from photography to teaching, but finds writing and illustrating children's books the most stimulating and satisfying.

"Books have always been very special to me," Mr. Weiss writes, "as sources of knowledge, as enlargers of experience, and as means of entertainment. Many of the books I bought and read and treasured as a youngster in school still rest in one of the many bookcases that are scattered through my home and which line the walls of the room were I work. One of the special shelves contains books that I have made myself, strictly for my own amusement. They are sketchbooks and photo albums, unfinished books of poetry, books full of doodles and random thoughts. Some have only a few pages. Others are fairly thick. The bindings are simple and were quickly done. Most of these books are dog-eared and worn from much use, and some, which were experimental, are crude and rather makeshift. But they were all great fun to make and to use. It is nice to have them close at hand where they can be thumbed through at idle moments or shown to friends. These are the kinds of books which *this book* is all about."